WORLD FOOTBALL SKILLS

BY DAVE SPURDENS

Published by Top That! Publishing plc
Copyright © 2010 Top That! Publishing plc
Tide Mill Way, Woodbridge, Suffolk, IP12 1AP, UK
www.topthatpublishing.com
Top That! is a registered trademark of Top That! Publishing plc

CONTENTS

INTRODUCTION

In the last decade football has changed. The game has become more skilful, at every level. Despite the increased levels of fitness and speed, players have found a way of entertaining fans and giving themselves a deeper level of self-satisfaction in their mastery of techniques and skills.

At every level, players today are willing to be more experimental and adventurous with the ball. Even recently, since the enormous talents of Ronaldo came to our shores, fans have adjusted their tolerance levels of what is permissible in the game.

When Ronaldo's high-speed step-over moves were first seen there was a reluctance to appreciate exactly how skilful and inventive his forays into enemy territory were. Today, players, whatever standard of football they are playing, strive to emulate him and fans thirst for his spectacular brand of football magic.

It is commonplace to see players juggling the ball or moving forward without the ball touching the ground in a game situation. Passes behind the standing foot, flicks and swivel kicks are common and variations of techniques and surfaces in trapping and controlling the ball, proliferate.

Thigh and chest skills are increasingly used to control the ball as an alternative to just getting rid of it for the sake of territorial advantage. A new premium has been placed on the importance of keeping the ball.

Possession can only be retained, in a competitive situation, by players who have honed their control techniques and have risen to a new level of disguise and craft.

The players in this book are all stars at the centre of the world stage. They are masters of the ball. They have the panache that can set the game alight and bring thousands of fans to their feet with a moment of creative genius. By following the step-by-step instructions of their signature moves, you will raise your game to a whole new level!

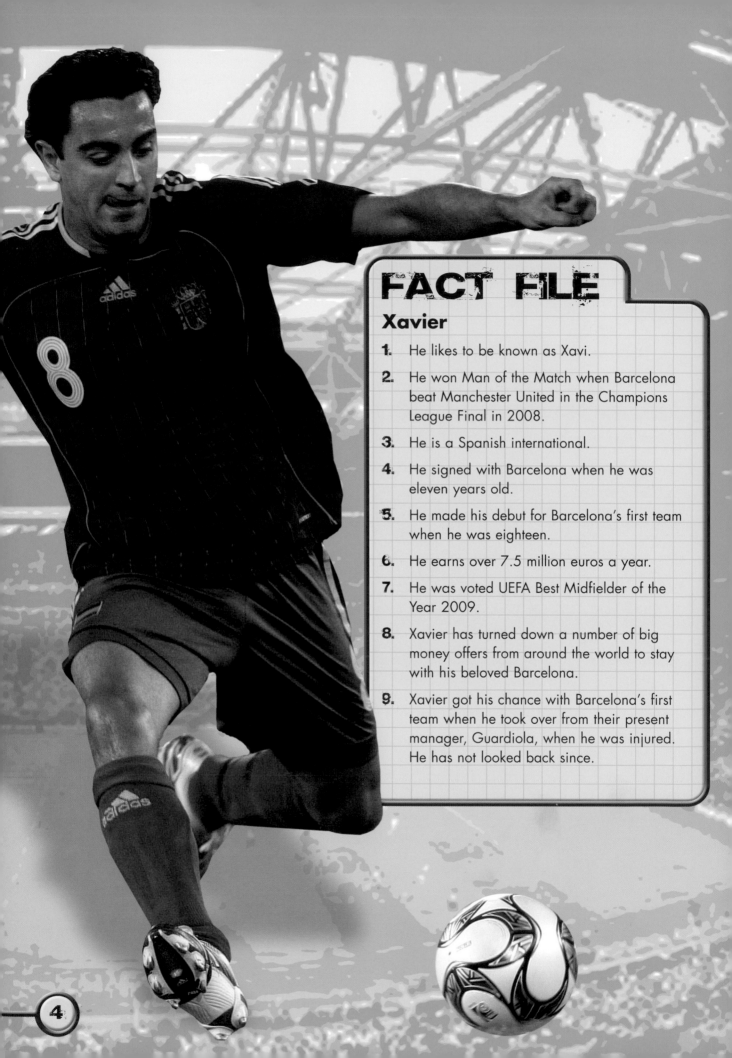

FACT FILE

Xavier

1. He likes to be known as Xavi.

2. He won Man of the Match when Barcelona beat Manchester United in the Champions League Final in 2008.

3. He is a Spanish international.

4. He signed with Barcelona when he was eleven years old.

5. He made his debut for Barcelona's first team when he was eighteen.

6. He earns over 7.5 million euros a year.

7. He was voted UEFA Best Midfielder of the Year 2009.

8. Xavier has turned down a number of big money offers from around the world to stay with his beloved Barcelona.

9. Xavier got his chance with Barcelona's first team when he took over from their present manager, Guardiola, when he was injured. He has not looked back since.

XAVIER
TOP FOOT TRAP OR CATCH

A Spanish midfield general par-excellence. Xavier's impeccable first touch is the launching pad for his many probing forages into enemy territory. This is one of the skills that are the platform for his powerful advancement.

Step 1: The two essential components of this skill are balance and keeping your eye on the ball. Make sure that you are balanced before you begin.

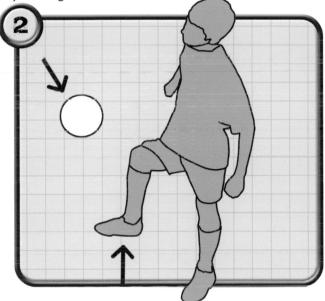

Step 2: As the ball drops you must watch its flight right into the controlling surface, which, in this case, is the top of the foot in the shoelaces area.

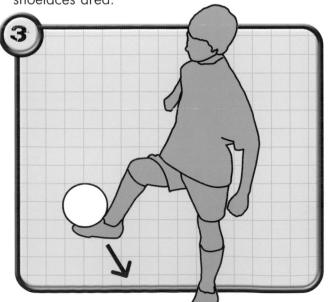

Step 3: Extend the controlling foot towards the ball with the knee flexed and the top of the foot offering a very level platform.

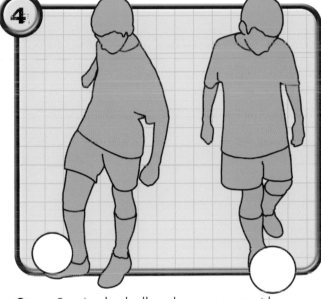

Step 4: As the ball makes contact with your foot, move it downwards. This will stop the ball from bouncing off your foot.

Step 5: At this point there are three options: (a) to catch the ball by arching your foot back and pincering the ball between your foot and shin. (b) To let the ball drop off your foot, onto the ground, ready for distribution or a forward run in possession, or (c) to move the ball off sideways as a pass to another player (this is best done to the outside of the controlling foot and can be clumsy if moved to the inside.).

FACT FILE

Kaká

1. Kaká's first love as a sports-mad child, up to the age of fifteen, was tennis.

2. He was the youngest ambassador ever appointed to the United Nations World Food Programme.

3. Kaká's brother, Rodrigo, known as Digão, is also a professional footballer.

4. When he was eighteen, Kaká suffered a serious, career threatening, spinal injury in a swimming pool accident.

5. Kaká attributed his recovery to God and has since given a great deal of his income to the church.

6. He began his career at the age of eight with São Paulo.

7. Silvio Berlusconi once described his signing fee of 8.5 million euros as 'peanuts'.

8. In 2007 Kaká won the coveted Ballon d'Or and was FIFA World Player of the Year.

9. He was named in Times Magazine as among the World's 100 Most Influential People.

10. It was reported that Manchester City made a bid of over one hundred million pounds for him.

KAKÁ
DRIBBLING USING BOTH OUTSIDE FOOT SURFACES

The legendary Brazilian has, for many years, thrilled millions of football enthusiasts with his skills at club level and for his country. He is one of those players who make smooth movement look effortless and much of this is due to his perfect touch and outside of the foot techniques.

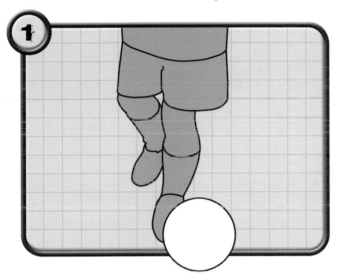

Step 1: Start by pushing the ball forwards using the outside of your dominant foot.

Step 2: As you start to run, move your body across the ball, in a smooth rhythm, maintaining control of the ball by using both outside surfaces of your feet.

Step 3: Ensure that the ball stays close to you. It should never be any further from your feet than a metre.

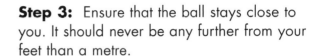

Step 4: After a great deal of practice you will be able to run with the ball and keep your head up to look for passing or shooting opportunities.

PRO TIP
Set up a series of four cones, or other items that you have to hand, one metre apart and practise dribbling in a straight line around them.

FACT FILE

David Villa

1. Villa's nickname is El Guaje ('The Kid').

2. He played in the 2006 FIFA World Cup and in UEFA Euro 2008, where he was top scorer with four goals.

3. He has scored over 140 goals in his career, making him one of the most prolific scorers in world football history.

4. One Spanish team that Villa had a trial for thought he was too short and lacked ability.

5. Manchester United have been linked with a fifty million pound, double swoop, for David Villa and David Silva, another Valencia forward.

6. Villa joined Valencia in 2005 for a fee of 12 million euros.

7. Barcelona and Real Madrid both made bids of 42 million euros for Villa in October 2009, which were turned down.

8. The year after he joined Valencia they won the Copa del Rey and Villa scored 25 goals for his team that season.

9. At the age of four, Villa broke his leg and there were doubts about him participating in any sport in the future.

10. Villa wanted to give up football when he was fourteen, but his father refused to let him quit. He went on to join UP Langrea, a local team, and from there he has never looked back.

DAVID VILLA
SOLE CONTROL

A Spanish striker with a prolific goal scoring rate, second only to compatriot Raúl, Villa's success in the box is due to his quick reactions and unexpected moves. One of the techniques he has frequently used to confuse opponents is the use of the sole as a controlling surface and a way to move the ball away from interception.

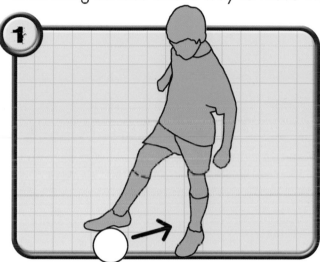

Step 1: Place the sole of your foot on the uppermost point of the ball.

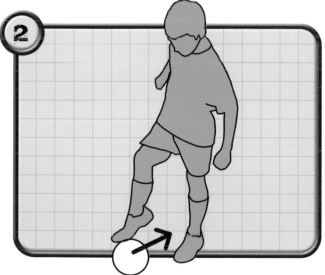

Step 2: Pull the ball back towards you and then quickly move it (in any direction) away from your marker.

PRO TIP
Do not stretch to gain control of the ball and frequently adjust the position of your standing foot to maintain your balance.

Step 3: Alternatively, run your sole over the top of the ball and pull the ball to the side.

Step 4: The sole pull can also be used as a stalling tactic while you are waiting for back-up from your teammates.

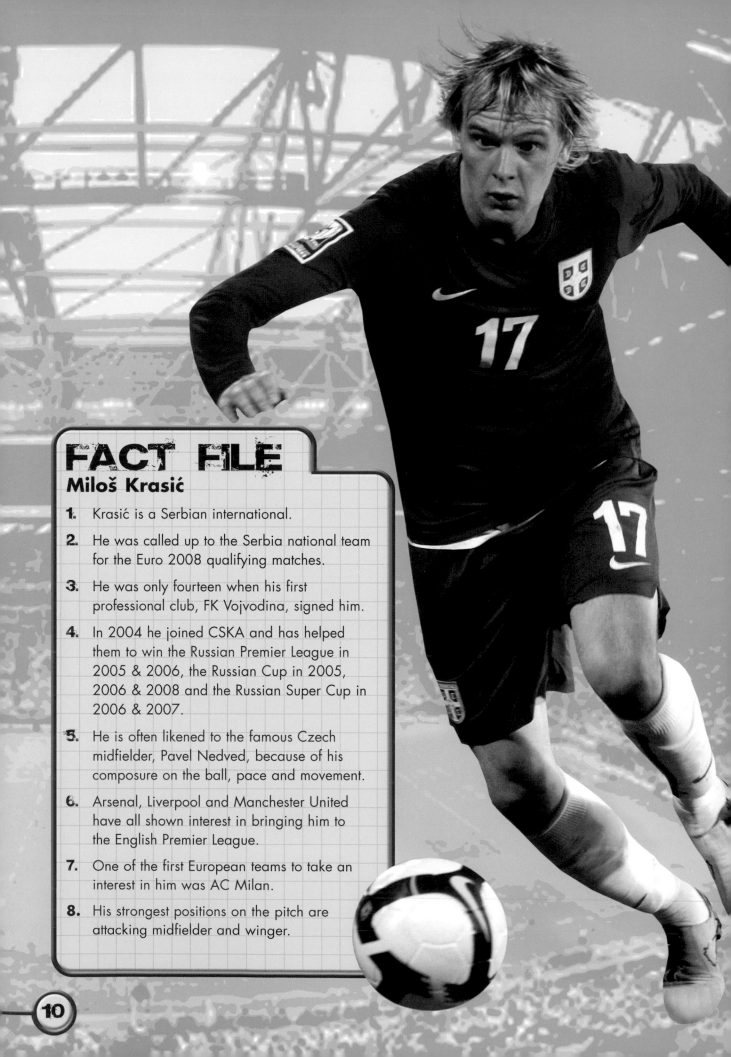

FACT FILE

Miloš Krasić

1. Krasić is a Serbian international.

2. He was called up to the Serbia national team for the Euro 2008 qualifying matches.

3. He was only fourteen when his first professional club, FK Vojvodina, signed him.

4. In 2004 he joined CSKA and has helped them to win the Russian Premier League in 2005 & 2006, the Russian Cup in 2005, 2006 & 2008 and the Russian Super Cup in 2006 & 2007.

5. He is often likened to the famous Czech midfielder, Pavel Nedved, because of his composure on the ball, pace and movement.

6. Arsenal, Liverpool and Manchester United have all shown interest in bringing him to the English Premier League.

7. One of the first European teams to take an interest in him was AC Milan.

8. His strongest positions on the pitch are attacking midfielder and winger.

MILOŠ KRASIĆ

THIGH CONTROL AND PASS

The thigh control technique or pass is a skill that allows a player to retain possession or gain advantage when the flight of the ball dictates that this is the best surface to use. A player's unique position at the time of needing to control the ball means that to use other surfaces, such as the chest or the feet, would throw the player off-balance. Great players always seem to select the right body surface at the right time.

Step 1: Try, as much as possible, to get into the line of flight of the ball.

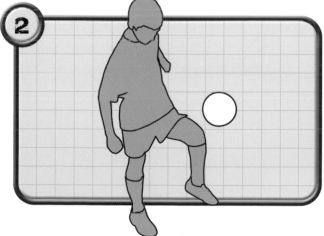

Step 2: As the ball nears you, prepare to extend your thigh up towards the ball.

PRO TIP

The skill has a greater chance of success, the less time you are balancing on one foot.

Step 3: If you are going to pass first time using your thigh, extend the surface towards the ball, at the point of contact.

Step 4: It the pass is going straight ahead, no body adjustments are needed, but if it is going to the side, your controlling thigh will need to be pointed towards the area you are aiming at.

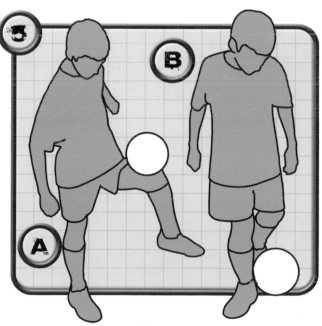

Step 5: If you are controlling the ball with your thigh to move it to another surface, the movement on contact is upwards for the chest and head (A). If you are re-directing the ball to your feet, your thigh needs to fall away at the moment of contact (B).

FACT FILE

Dimitar Berbatov

1. Fans in Bulgaria call Berbatov by his nicknames, which are 'Berbo' and 'Berba'.

2. His first club was CSKA Sofia. Berbatov was with them from 1999 to 2001. He scored 25 goals in 50 matches.

3. He joined German side, Bayer Leverkusen, in 2001 and played for them until 2006. He scored 69 goals in 154 matches.

4. He joined Tottenham Hotspur in 2006 and scored 27 goals in 70 matches.

5. He is a highly capped Bulgarian international.

6. He has scored more international goals than his legendary countryman, Hristo Stoichkov.

7. Berbatov was awarded the Bulgarian Footballer of the Year Award in 2002, 2004, 2005 and 2007.

8. Berbatov was awarded the Premier League Player of the Month Award while at Tottenham.

9. Berbatov's mother always dreamt of her son playing for Newcastle.

10. When Berbatov was a child, he wore a Newcastle shirt, bearing the number 9 of his hero, Alan Shearer, as a pyjama top.

DIMITAR BERBATOV
CHEST CONTROL AND PASS

More and more, we are seeing the use of the chest pass in the modern game. As a creative striker, who often drops deep when there are pressures of limited time and space, Bulgarian international, Berbatov, knows it can sometimes mean the difference between retaining the ball or losing it.

1

Step 1: Like all skills, where the ball travels to you from height, it is essential to follow the path of the ball so that you are lined up to meet it with the chosen controlling surface of your body.

2

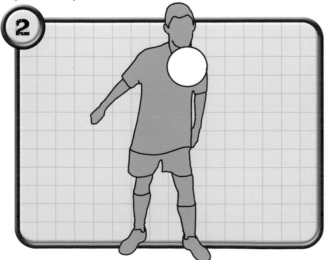

Step 2: As the ball arrives at your chest, your next move is conditioned by the direction

you want the ball to travel in and the distance. If the intended pass is straight, your chest should be moved towards the ball and in the direction it needs to travel.

3

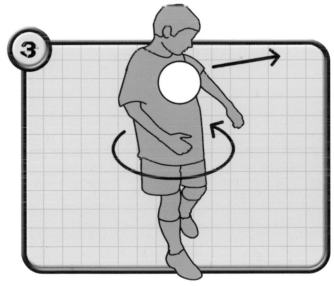

Step 3: If you intend to pass at an angle, you must turn from the hips, in the direction of the pass, as soon as the ball makes contact.

13

FACT FILE

Wayne Rooney

1. At the age of ten, Wayne Rooney became a youth team player for Everton (in 1996). In 2002 he started playing in the first team.

2. Rooney became the youngest ever goalscorer in the Premier League in 2002.

3. He played 67 games for Everton's first team and scored 15 goals.

4. Rooney is an England national player with a prolific scoring record.

5. Manchester United paid 25.6 million pounds for Rooney in 2004.

6. His England debut was at the UEFA Euro 2004 and he briefly became the competition's youngest goalscorer.

7. Rooney's childhood hero was Duncan Ferguson, the Scotland and Everton striker.

8. Rooney once wore a t-shirt under his Everton jersey that read, 'Once a Blue, Always a Blue'.

9. Rooney famously broke his metatarsal bone during the 2005/2006 season.

WAYNE ROONEY
SHOVEL PASS

The Manchester United striker has used this skill to great profit on many occasions, especially when space is at a premium and an overlap has been performed by a supporting player.

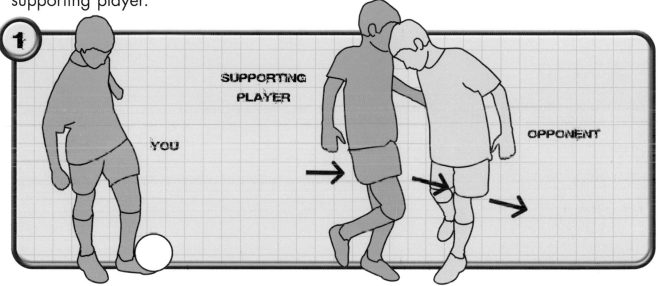

Step 1: Control the ball and then come to a halt. Then, wait for your supporting player to pass in front of your opponent (overlap). If necessary, drag the ball back to retain possession using 'sole control' (see page 8-9).

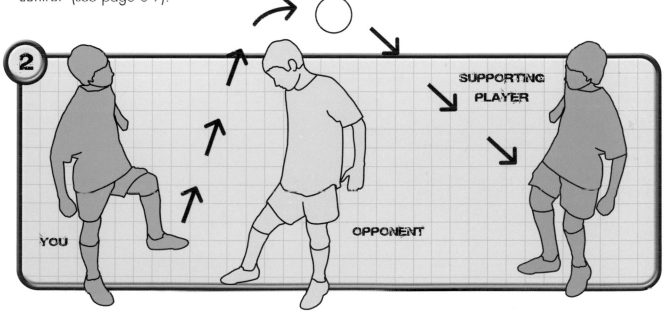

Step 2: Place the toe and shoelaces of your boot under the ball and flex from the knee, lifting the ball forwards and upwards, so that it passes over the head of your opponent and onto your supporting player, who is now waiting to receive your shovel pass.

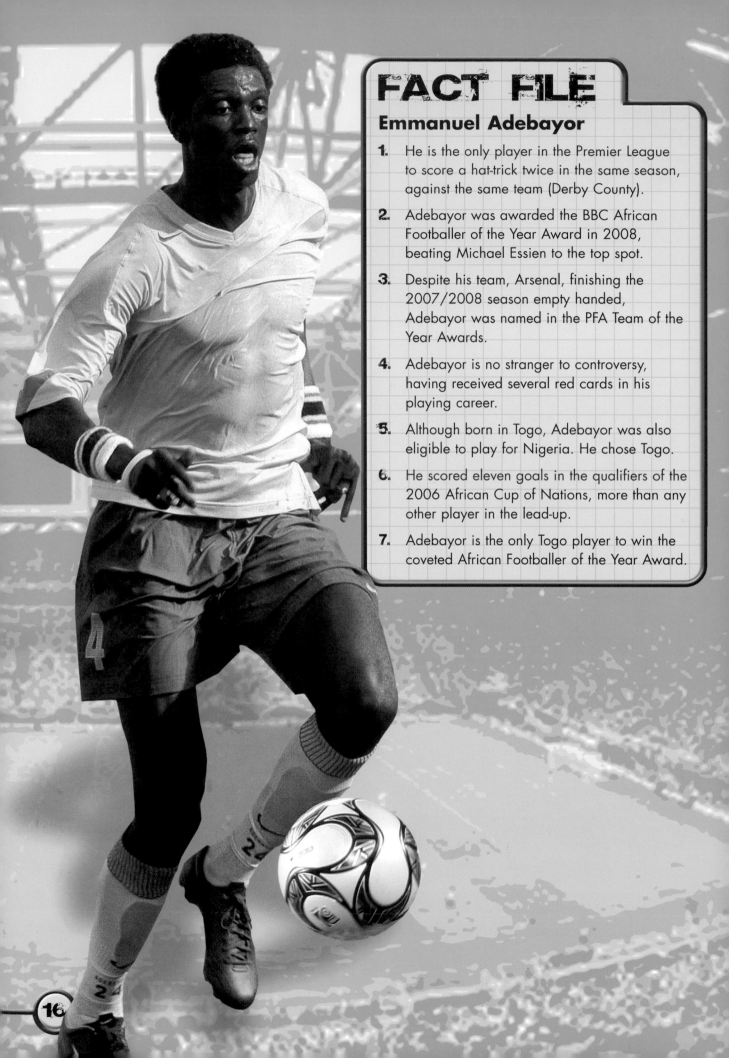

FACT FILE

Emmanuel Adebayor

1. He is the only player in the Premier League to score a hat-trick twice in the same season, against the same team (Derby County).

2. Adebayor was awarded the BBC African Footballer of the Year Award in 2008, beating Michael Essien to the top spot.

3. Despite his team, Arsenal, finishing the 2007/2008 season empty handed, Adebayor was named in the PFA Team of the Year Awards.

4. Adebayor is no stranger to controversy, having received several red cards in his playing career.

5. Although born in Togo, Adebayor was also eligible to play for Nigeria. He chose Togo.

6. He scored eleven goals in the qualifiers of the 2006 African Cup of Nations, more than any other player in the lead-up.

7. Adebayor is the only Togo player to win the coveted African Footballer of the Year Award.

EMMANUEL ADEBAYOR
OUTSIDE FOOT BENT HALF VOLLEY

This is a shot or, sometimes a long pass, that has crowds gasping and, quite often, goalkeepers stretching for the ball that is just outside of their grasp. It is a technique that Adebayor has mastered and one which contributes greatly to his high goal tally as a striker.

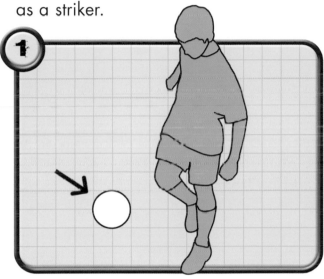

Step 1: It is crucial to keep your eye on the ball when performing this skill. The moment of contact is precisely when the ball meets the ground and there is no margin of error!

the ball (as Step 2). If you are looking for distance or height, then you must lean back.

Step 3: The outside of your foot between the shoelaces and the little toe should be the contact point and a follow-through with your kicking leg will ensure greater power.

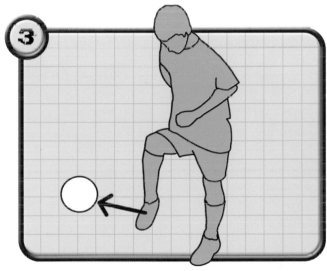

Step 2: To send the ball in a straight or low trajectory, your body should be straight or over

PRO TIP
The more to the side of the ball you are, on contact, the greater the swerve on your shot.

FACT FILE

Carlos Tévez

1. Carlos Tévez is one of the first players to be owned by a company (Media Sports Investments) and play in the Premier League.

2. He was described by Diego Maradona as the 'Argentine prophet for the 21st century'.

3. Tévez is a member of the Argentina national side.

4. Tévez was raised in Fuerte Apache, a crime ridden area of Buenos Aires.

5. His nickname is 'El Apache', due to the place he grew up.

6. The scar on Tévez's face was caused when he was accidentally scalded, at home, with boiling water. He was in intensive care with 'third degree burns' for two months.

7. In 2004 Tévez transferred from his first club, Boca Juniors to Corinthians of Brazil for a fee of 13.7 million pounds. He also signed a five year deal with Media Sports Investments. It was the biggest transfer deal ever in South America.

8. In 2005 he was voted the Brazilian Player of the Year. He was the first non-Brazilian to win the award since 1976.

9. Tévez joined West Ham from Corinthians in a joint deal with Javier Mascherano. They cost 12 million pounds each.

10. In 2007 Tévez scored the winning goal against Manchester United to ensure West Ham's controversial survival in the Premier League.

CARLOS TÉVEZ
OUTSIDE FOOT BENT VOLLEY

Tévez has gained the reputation, at club and country level, as a forward who can turn a half-chance into a goal. Because he fights so hard to get and retain the ball, many of his shooting skills are executed when he appears to be off-balance. This skill is an integral part of his shooting armoury.

Step 1: A volley can be used when the ball is at any reachable height. The positioning of your body is dependent on the height of the ball travelling towards you. The lower the ball the more extended your kicking leg should be.

Step 2: Quite often the high trajectory ball will require your body to 'fall away' to enable a solid connection with your outside foot.

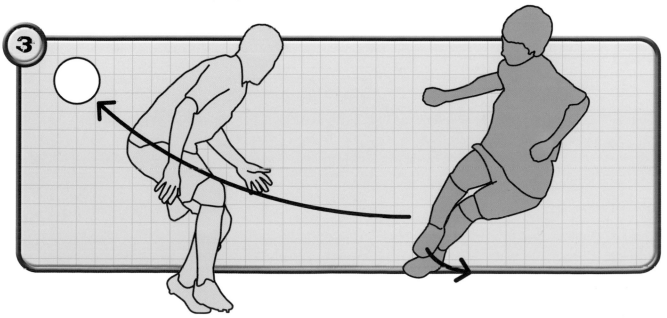

Step 3: For maximum swerve, allow your kicking foot to follow through, across the front of your standing foot.

FACT FILE

Shunsuke Nakamura

1. Nakamura's first club was Yokahama F. Marinos, where he played from 1997 to 2002. They are the company club of Nissan Motors.

2. In 2007, while playing for Celtic, he won the Scottish Professional Footballers Association Players' Player of the Year Award and the Scottish Football Writers' Player of the Year Award.

3. He won the Celtic Fans Player of the Year Award and the SPL Goal of the Season Award for one of his goals scored against Dundee United.

4. Nakamura's international career suffered when Phillipe Troussier managed Japan and he was frequently left out of squads by the Frenchman.

5. His international career was resurrected when Zico, the famous Brazilian footballer took over, he described Nakamura as, '... the soul of our midfield'.

SHUNSUKE NAKAMURA
BEHIND STANDING FOOT TRAP

This skill can wrong-foot an opponent and gain an advantage for the player with the ball. It is especially helpful when the flight of the ball changes while in the air and saves an awkward re-adjustment of your body shape.

Step 1: At the time of contact your chest should be facing the flight path of the ball.

Step 2: Your trapping leg should be bent at the knee and crossed behind your standing leg ready to accomodate the ball.

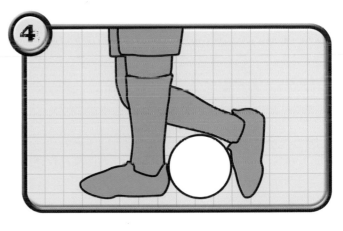

Step 4: The extent to which the ball is 'killed' is determined by the angle of the heel. If your heel is inclined and in a forward position, the ball will be trapped completely.

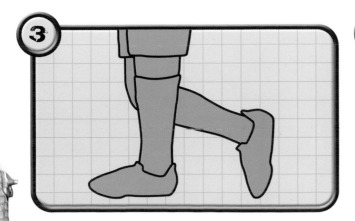

Step 3: At the point of contact, the toe of your playing leg should be touching the ground so the ball can be trapped between the ground and the inside arch of your foot.

Step 5: If you want the ball to spin out of the trap in order to move on with the ball, keep your body in an upright position and increase the angle of your heel.

FACT FILE

Cesc Fàbregas

1. Fàbregas was a trainee with Barcelona, and was signed by Arsenal at the age of sixteen, quickly establishing himself in the Arsenal first team.

2. He was Arsenal's youngest ever first team player when he played in a League Cup tie at home to Rotherham.

3. Fàbregas got his first team break at Arsenal because of an injury to Patrick Vieira.

4. Fàbregas was taken to watch his first match at Camp Nou by his grandfather when he was just nine months old.

5. He played many games for Barcelona's youth teams and was a prolific goalscorer, netting over 30 a season.

6. Fàbregas starred in his own TV programme called 'The Cesc Fàbregas Show: Nike Live'. It was shown on Sky Sports in 2008.

7. Fàbregas has said that while Patrick Vieira was his role model and mentor, the man he styles his game on is Joseph Pep Guardiola.

CESC FABREGAS
INSIDE FOOT RIDE

As a supremo of midfield domination, Fàbregas employs every skill in the book that affords him economy of movement and unassailable possession. This is a skill that allows him to move from receiving a pass with his back to the goal when he wants to attack, having turned to face the opposition goal.

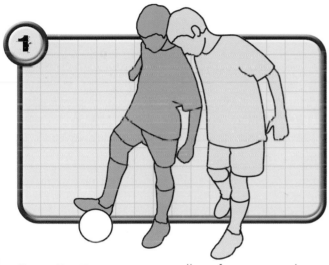

Step 1: Turn your controlling foot out so that the inside instep is presented squarely to the ball.

Step 2: Extend your foot towards the ball and, on impact, withdraw it to cushion the ball. Then, pivot on your standing foot and bring the ball around as you do so. Both parts of this step should be done in one fluid motion, keeping your body in between the ball and your opponent.

Step 3: You will now be facing the opposite direction to which you received the ball, with the ball 'glued' to your controlling foot.

FACT FILE

Tomas Rosicky

1. Rosicky's nickname is 'The Little Mozart'. He was given this name while playing in Germany, due to his ability to orchestrate play on the pitch.

2. Rosicky was transferred to Borussia Dortmund for 14.5 million euros, a Bundesliga record transfer fee and the most Sparta Prague had ever received for a player.

3. He played 126 games for Borussia Dortmund and scored 19 goals.

4. Rosicky made his debut for the Czech Republic when he was nineteen years of age against the Republic of Ireland.

5. At the beginning of the 2006/07 season, he was made captain of the Czech Republic side, taking over from the legendary Pavel Nedved.

6. When he was signed by Arsenal, his transfer fee was kept secret and is still not known today.

THOMAS ROSICKY
HEEL PASS TO THE SIDE

A great skill for changing the direction of the game and creating space. It has the element of surprise and allows the player performing it to disguise their intentions up to the moment they execute it. Rosicky's game is built on keeping markers guessing what he is going to do next and this is one technique that ensures he preserves that reputation.

Step 1: When you are under pressure from a defender, identify a teammate to whom you can make a square pass.

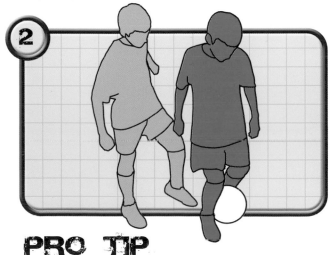

Step 2: Play the ball forward, and turn your playing foot outwards and to the outside of the ball.

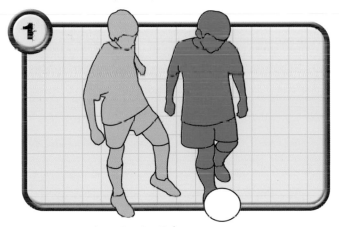

PRO TIP
This is a good pass anywhere in the attacking half of the pitch, but is especially effective when used on the flanks.

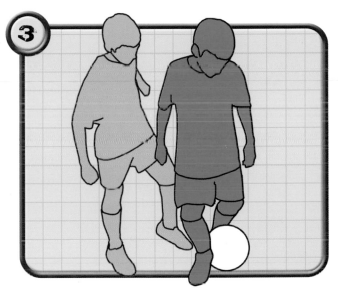

Step 3: Aim your heel at the ball, sending it across your standing foot.

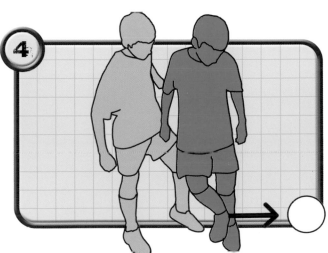

Step 4: The extent to which the playing foot is 'cocked' determines the power of the pass and the distance it can travel. Practise this skill so that you can weight the pass correctly.

FACT FILE

Didier Drogba

1. Drogba was born in Abidjan, Cote d'Ivoire, but started his career as a youth team player with French amateur side Levallois-Perret.

2. In 1998 he joined French top-flight club Le Mans, and stayed there until 2002. He made 64 appearances and scored 12 goals.

3. Strangely, his next move was to Guingamp, a Ligue 2 side. Drogba spent just one season at Guingamp before moving to Marseille. He made 45 appearances and scored 20 goals.

4. Drogba did not sign his first professional contract until he was 21.

5. Marseille paid Guingamp 3.3 million pounds for Drogba in 2003 and he scored 19 goals in his first season.

6. Marseille made a handsome profit on Drogba when they sold him to Chelsea for 24 million pounds in 2004.

7. He is captain of his national team, Cote d'Ivoire.

8. In the 2006/07 season he was the Premier League's top scorer with 20 goals.

9. Drogba scored the winning goals in the 2007 League Cup and the FA Cup Final.

DIDIER DROGBA
PASS RECEIVED AND BALL
THROUGH LEGS WITH INSIDE FOOT TURN

Didier Drogba has earned the reputation for being the most difficult striker in the world to mark and control. Moving the ball out of a marker's reach is his speciality and this is one of the skills that makes him such an elusive player.

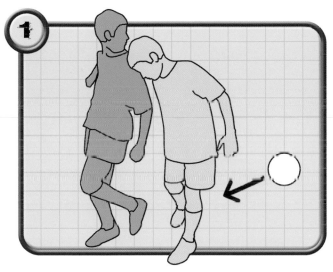

Step 1: You must be sideways on when the ball is played to you. However, by the time it arrives, you must be looking backwards at the oncoming ball and running towards the goal.

Step 2: The ball must pass between your legs from behind, which makes it very difficult for a marker to attack the ball without committing a foul.

Step 3: Once the ball has passed through your legs, use the inside of either foot to control the ball and change the direction of the ball and your own progress forward. This will throw your marker off balance.

27

FACT FILE

Eduardo

1. Eduardo was born in Rio de Janeiro, Brazil.

2. He was spotted playing for a youth team by Dinamo Zagreb's scouts and was asked to join their youth programme in Croatia.

3. Eduardo made his first team debut with Dinamo in the 2001/2002 season.

4. He scored 10 goals in 15 matches in that first season and was being talked of as a boy wonder in Croatia and elsewhere.

5. In 2004, 2006, and 2007 he was named Best Player in the Croatian League.

6. In the 2006/07 season he netted 18 goals in 18 games, including three braces and a hat-trick.

7. Eduardo became the most prolific goalscorer in Croatian football of all time, breaking a 13 year-old record held by Goran Vlaovic. He scored 29 goals in one season.

8. Eduardo joined Arsenal in the Premier League, for a fee that was undisclosed, but was probably in the region of 7.5 million pounds.

9. Eduardo suffered one of the worst injuries ever seen in English football in a game against Birmingham City when he broke his left fibula. It was thought, at the time, that he might never play again.

10. Eduardo became a Croatian national in 2002.

EDUARDO
CURLING INSIDE FOOT SHOT

This Brazilian born striker has all the subtlety and craft about his game that you would associate with his birthplace. Not least among his many attributes is his ability to bend strikes on goal, making it difficult for goalkeepers to know exactly where the ball is going.

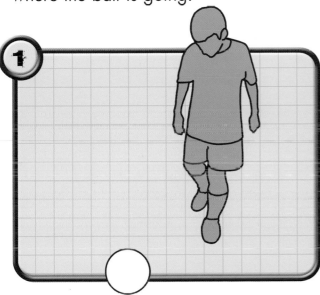

Step 1: Short run-up. Eduardo has perfected the art of disguising his curling shots, as he does not take a big run-up when unleashing a shot from a set-piece or when he shoots while the ball is in play.

Step 3: The most important factor to remember is that the further to the outside of the ball you make contact, the greater the 'curl', you will achieve.

Step 2: The ball must be kicked on the outside surface, using the inside instep at the base of the big toe.

PRO TIP
The degree of swerve can also be increased by using the area around the ball of the toe, starting the contact from the back, outside of the ball.

FACT FILE

Teko Modise

1. Teko Modise was born in the Johannesburg township of Soweto.

2. His first club, where he played youth soccer, was Ria Stars, who were bought out by the league for 8 million rand to reduce fixture congestion.

3. Teko's first club in the Premier League was Supersport United, based in Pretoria and known as Matsatsantsa (The Swanky Boys). The club has one of the most successful youth academies in the country. They have a partnership arrangement with Tottenham Hotspur.

4. He was voted Mvela Golden League Player of the Season whilst playing for a team called City Pillars.

5. He was appointed ambassador for the 2010 World Cup by McDonalds and Coca Cola, Telcom and Samsung.

6. He was part of the South African squad that won the 2007 COSAFA Cup.

7. In 2009 he was awarded the Budweiser Man of the Match Award in the opening game of the Confederations Cup.

8. He was Premier Soccer League Player of the Year in 2009.

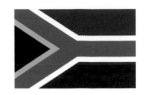

TEKO MODISE
THE OVERHEAD SCISSORS KICK

Lithe, agile and fast, this exciting South African forward is ideally equipped for this skill and while it is not a big part of his game, Modise has used it to stick the ball in the back of the net. It was once called the 'Bicycle Kick', because it resembles the action of a cyclist with one leg rotating after the other.

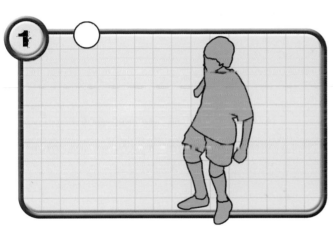

Step 1: Position yourself beneath the ball with your back to the target. Your legs should be bent at the knees ready to make an upward thrust.

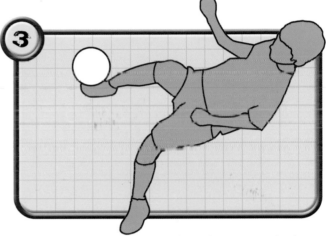

Step 3: Extend your kicking leg towards the ball and rotate your hips so that your kicking leg moves across your body to meet the ball.

Step 2: Take-off is launched from your non-kicking foot and an upward thrust of the upper body. Your body will naturally fall back into position as gravity takes hold.

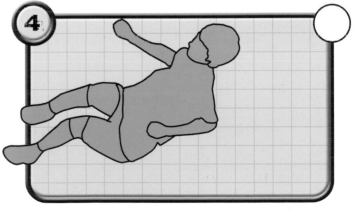

Step 4: Strike the ball with the laces area of your boot.

PRO TIP
It is essential to plan how and where you are going to fall, as there is a danger of injury with this skill.

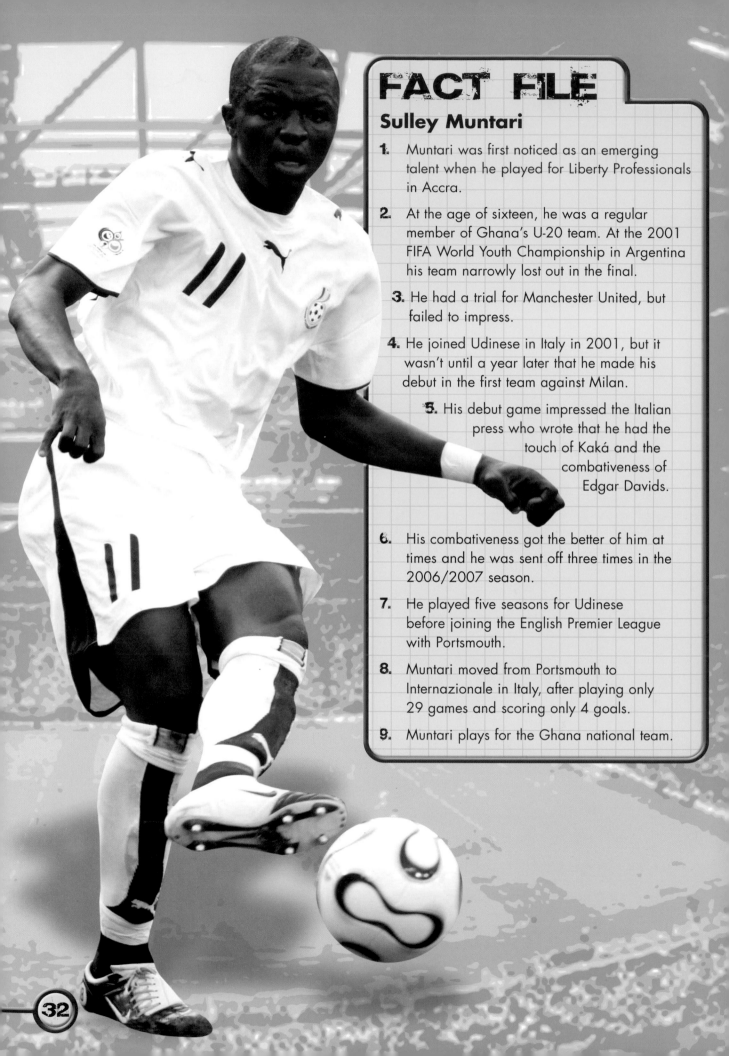

FACT FILE

Sulley Muntari

1. Muntari was first noticed as an emerging talent when he played for Liberty Professionals in Accra.

2. At the age of sixteen, he was a regular member of Ghana's U-20 team. At the 2001 FIFA World Youth Championship in Argentina his team narrowly lost out in the final.

3. He had a trial for Manchester United, but failed to impress.

4. He joined Udinese in Italy in 2001, but it wasn't until a year later that he made his debut in the first team against Milan.

5. His debut game impressed the Italian press who wrote that he had the touch of Kaká and the combativeness of Edgar Davids.

6. His combativeness got the better of him at times and he was sent off three times in the 2006/2007 season.

7. He played five seasons for Udinese before joining the English Premier League with Portsmouth.

8. Muntari moved from Portsmouth to Internazionale in Italy, after playing only 29 games and scoring only 4 goals.

9. Muntari plays for the Ghana national team.

SULLEY MUNTARI
PASS FROM TOP FOOT CATCH

An attacking midfielder, Muntari is noted for his calmness in possession and it is his first touch skills that give him this air of confidence on the ball. This is a 'luxury' skill, but in tight situations it can confuse opponents and certainly catches the eye of spectators everywhere. This skill is sometimes called the 'sling shot'.

Step 1: Follow the trajectory of the ball when it is in the air and position yourself so that you can trap the ball between your shin and the top of your kicking foot.

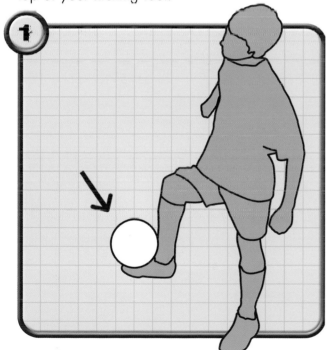

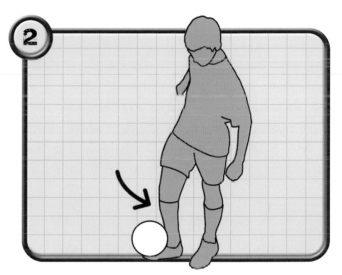

Step 2: As the ball connects with your shin and the top of your kicking foot, immediately pull your kicking leg backwards to take the pace off the ball.

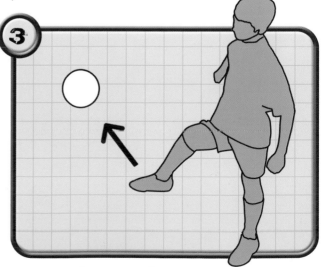

PRO TIP
This shot or pass can be sent in any direction and can even be used to kick the ball backwards over your head.

Step 3: Thrust your foot forwards, extending from the knee, to unleash an explosive shot or long-range pass.

FACT FILE

Ronaldinho

1. Ronaldinho is Portuguese for 'Little Ronaldo' and he is also known by his nickname 'Gaucho' to distinguish him from his Brazilian teammate Ronaldo.

2. Ronaldinho's father was a shipyard worker and a footballer, but tragically died from a heart attack while swimming in the family pool when Ronaldinho was eight.

3. His brother, Roberto, was a professional footballer who played for Gremio, a top-flight team in Brazil. Unfortunately, his career was cut short by injury.

4. Ronaldinho loved playing beach football and he first came to the attention of the media when he scored all 23 goals in a 23–0 victory against a local team.

5. Ronaldinho is married to a Brazilian dancer, Janaina Mendes and they have a son who is named after Ronaldinho's father, Joao.

6. Arsenal expressed an interest in signing Ronaldinho, but when he could not obtain a work permit the deal fell through.

7. He played 44 times for Brazilian side Gremio and scored 21 goals, before signing for Paris Saint-Germain.

8. He played 55 games for PSG, scoring 17 goals, and then moved to Barcelona.

9. Barcelona signed Ronaldinho, outbidding Manchester United, with a fee of 32.5 million euros.

RONALDINHO
PASS WHILE LOOKING IN THE OPPOSITE DIRECTION

When Ronaldinho introduced this skill into his, already considerable, repertoire the Barcelona fans loved it. At first they gasped, then they cheered and then they laughed at the impudence of a player who was so skilful that he did not have to look in the direction he was playing the ball.

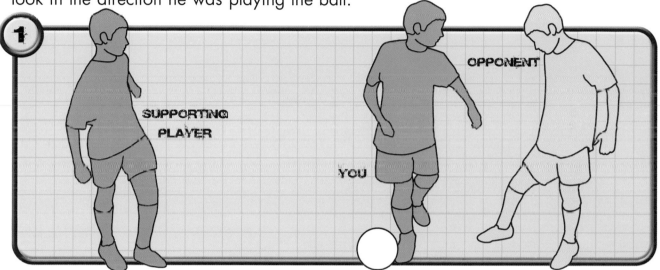

Step 1: Ronaldinho tends to have the ball on the outside surface of his dominant foot before he makes this move. If he has the ball on the outside of his right foot, and he knows a good and accurate pass is possible to the right, he looks to the left and suggests with all his body movement that the last thing he is going to do with the ball is play it right.

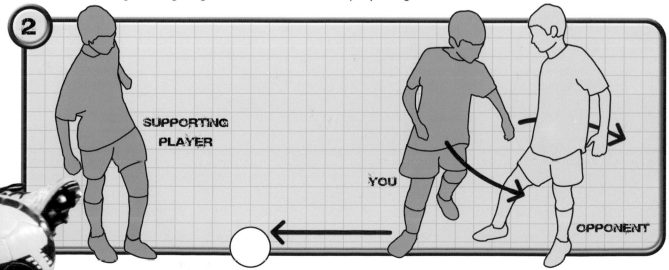

Step 2: Having looked to the left and moved his body to the left, he plays it right with the outside surface of his right foot. Practise this move to bring some Ronaldinho magic into your game!

FACT FILE

Frank Lampard

1. Lampard played 148 games for West Ham United and scored 24 goals.

2. Lampard's father, Frank Lampard Snr, played 660 games for West Ham as a left back and played four times for England. He finished his playing career at Southend United, which was then managed by Bobby Moore.

3. In 2005, Frank junior came second in both the Ballon d'Or and FIFA World Player of the Year Award.

4. After spending seven years at West Ham, Lampard moved to London rivals Chelsea for a fee of 11 million pounds.

5. He holds the club record of playing 164 consecutive Premier League games for Chelsea.

6. In 2008, after signing a new contract with Chelsea, Lampard established himself as the highest paid Premier League player at that time with a salary thought to be £140,000 a week.

7. Lampard was shown to have an unusually high IQ in a study by the Chelsea club doctor.

8. He is an England national player with a great goal scoring record.

9. After his mother died of pneumonia in 2008, Lampard's goal celebrations have been devoted to her memory, as he sinks to his knees and looks skywards.

FRANK LAMPARD
THE GLIDE DUMMY

The Chelsea and England midfielder uses this skill to make room for his fearsome strikes on goal.

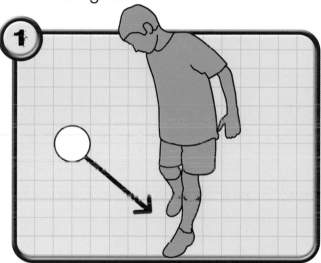

Step 1: Position your body diagonally so as to shield the incoming ball from your marker.

Step 2: Lift one of your feet as if to strike or control the ball.

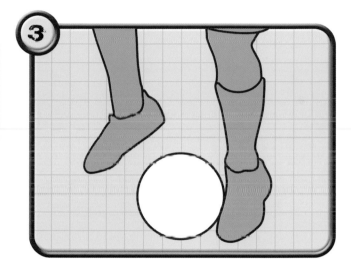

Step 3: Just before the point of contact, allow the ball to pass under your foot and through to the inside surface of your other foot.

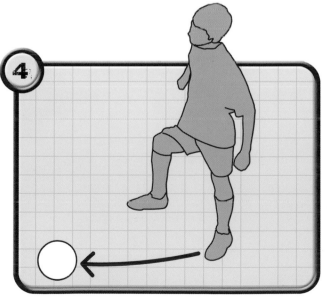

Step 4: Play the ball, with the inside surface of your foot, in the direction of the original pass, leaving your marker stranded.

FACT FILE

Mauro Camoranesi

1. Camoranesi was born in Buenos Aires, moved to Mexico to begin his professional career and also plays for Italy's national team.

2. He scored only one league goal in 13 games in his first season with Mexican Primera Division side Santos Laguna in a championship winning campaign.

3. He played one season for Santos Laguna, and had a brief spell with Uruguayan club, Montevideo Wanderers, before going back to Buenos Aires based side, Banfield. His next move was back to Mexico, where he signed for Cruz Azal, another Primera Division side. He made 79 appearances for Cruz Azal and scored 21 goals.

4. His next move to Verona, a Serie A side, was to shape his future commitment to Italian football. He spent two seasons with Verona, playing 51 games and scoring 7 goals.

5. In 2002 Camoranesi was signed on a co-ownership deal by Juventus for 4.8 million euros. A year later he was signed outright for an additional fee of 5 million euros.

6. In his first year at Juventus they won Serie A and the Italian Super Cup.

7. Camoranesi went on to be part of the side that won the Serie A league titles. However, the club was stripped of both these titles, as a result of a major scandal, which became known as the 'Calciopoli'. It saw the club relegated for their part in the scandal.

8. He is an Italian national player.

9. When criticised for not singing the words of the Italian National Anthem, Camoranesi said 'I feel Argentine, but I have defended the colours of Italy with dignity. That is something nobody can take away'.

MAURO CAMORANESI
THE PULL, PUSH AND SHOT

Mauro Camoranesi, the Juventus attacking midfielder has perfected the art of arriving in the box late and scoring, seemingly, impossible goals. This skilful raider is an infinite box of tricks when he is near the goal and this is one of his skills that often leaves defenders scratching their heads.

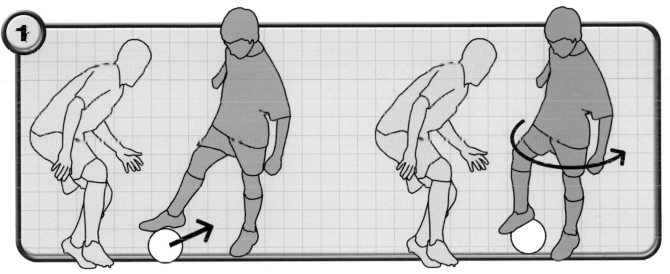

Step 1: When you have the ball at your feet, and are aware that a challenge is about to come in, pull the ball back from the challenge using the sole of your boot, and rotate your body in the direction of the ball, to make space for the shot.

Step 2: Use your other foot to push the ball, taking it past your opponent's back. Having evaded the challenge you can pass, continue your run or, as Camoranesi has on more than one occasion, shoot and score a goal.

FACT FILE

Robinho

1. Robinho was picked by Pelé as his 'heir-apparent', at only fifteen years of age.

2. He joined Santos, the team Pelé played for, when he was sixteen, and went on to lead them to their first title since Pelé was their star player.

3. He won one more title with Santos during his 111 appearances and scored 46 goals.

4. He won two more titles with Real Madrid, one 'Copa America', title with Brazil and two Confederation Cups.

5. Robinho was transferred to Real Madrid from Santos for 24 million euros.

6. In 2004, Robinho's mother was kidnapped by gunmen at her home, but was released six weeks later, unharmed, after an unspecified ransom was paid.

7. Robinho took over the number 10 shirt at Real Madrid that was previously worn by Luis Figo.

8. He made 37 appearances and scored 14 goals in his first season.

9. Fabio Capello thought that Robinho and David Beckham were too flashy and glamorous to be in his side and they spent months on the bench in the 2006/2007 season.

10. When Cappello left the club, Robinho and Beckham returned to the team and played a crucial role in achieving Real Madrid's thirtieth league title.

11. Robinho's transfer from Real Madrid to Manchester City, for 42.5 million euros, established him as one of the highest paid players in the English Premier League, on wages of £160,000 a week.

ROBINHO
ONE STEP OVER DUMMY FROM INSIDE THE BALL TO THE OUTSIDE

It's the must-learn skill and is being used by players all over the world since Ronaldo, the Portuguese forward, made this trick such a feature of his exciting game. Remember, the essential ingredients for this skill are pace and a close touch. Robinho, the Brazilian winger, has successfully integrated the skill into his game.

Step 1: Establish a good rhythm as you approach your marker. The ball should never be more than half a metre from your controlling foot.

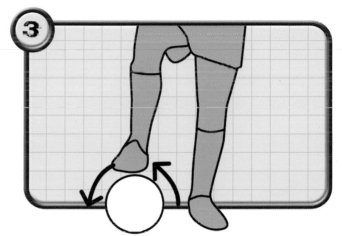

Step 2: Use the outside surface of the controlling foot to move the ball forward.

Step 3: As you approach your marker, the foot that is controlling the ball passes over the top of the ball from inside to outside, with no loss of pace as this movement is made.

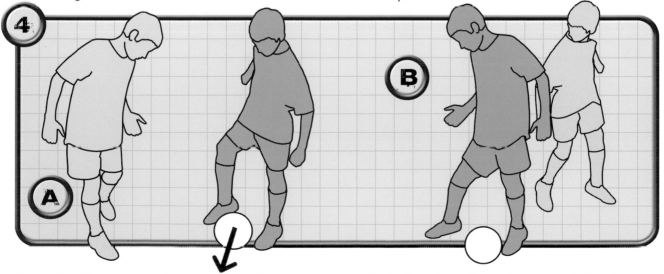

Step 4: The moment the dummying foot passes over the ball and lands on the ground (A), the ball should immediately be played towards your other foot (using either surface of the other foot) as you accelerate past your marker (B), taking immediate advantage of his movement in the wrong direction.

FACT FILE

Frank Ribéry

1. Ribéry spent the first four years of his career with four different French clubs. In 2005, he relocated to Turkey and signed a loan contract with Galatasaray.

2. At the end of the season, Ribéry moved back to France to play for Marseille. Galatasaray appealed and tried to sue the French club for taking Ribéry before his contract had terminated. In 2007, the courts ruled in Ribéry's favour and stated that his contract had been terminated on just grounds.

3. Ribéry smashed a club record for Bayern Munich in 2007, when they signed him for 25 million euros.

4. In 2008, Ribéry was named the 2007/2008 German Footballer of the Year.

5. Ribéry is a French national player. He earned his first cap in May 2006.

6. Fellow French player, Zinedine Zidane, called Ribéry the 'jewel of French football'.

7. When Ribéry was two, he and his family were involved in a serious car accident. Ribéry had facial injuries, which resulted in over a hundred stitches, leaving two scars down the right side of his face.

FRANCK RIBÉRY

STEP OVER FROM OUTSIDE TO INSIDE

Revered for his explosive pace, skill, boundless energy and excellent passing skills, Ribéry has risen to the status only enjoyed in France by players like Henry and Zidane. His use of the step-over skills, coupled with blistering speed, has made him one of the hottest properties on the European transfer market.

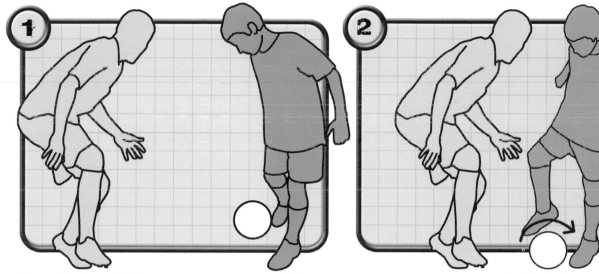

Step 1: As with the previous step-over skill, use the outside surface of your controlling foot to move the ball towards your marker.

Step 2: As you move the ball closer to your marker, pass your controlling foot over the ball from the outside to the inside.

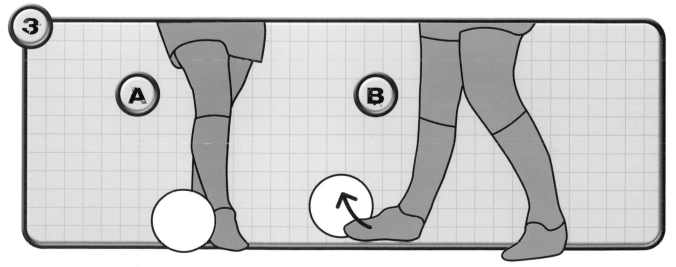

Step 3: As your foot touches down to the inside of the ball (A), the outside surface of the same foot makes contact with the ball, enabling you to move past your marker in the opposite direction (B).

FACT FILE

Cristiano Ronaldo

1. Cristiano Ronaldo dos Santos Aveiro was born on 5 February 1985 in Funchal, Madeira (a Portuguese island in the Atlantic Ocean).

2. At the age of eight, Ronaldo played for an amateur team called Andorinha.

3. At the age of fifteen, Ronaldo was diagnosed with a heart condition. Fortunately, he had an operation, which solved the problem.

4. Ronaldo was signed to Manchester United for 12.24 million pounds at the end of 2002/03 season.

5. He earned his first cap for Portugal in a 1–0 victory against Kazakhstan in August 2003.

6. During his time at Manchester United, the club won the Premier League (2006/07, 2007/08, 2008//09), FA Cup (2003/04), League Cup (2005/06, 2008/09), FA Community Shield (2007), UEFA Champions League (2007/08), and FIFA Club World Cup (2008). Ronaldo was instrumental in the club's success.

7. Ronaldo was the first Premier League player to be named the FIFA World Player of the Year.

8. Ronaldo was the second-highest scorer in the FIFA 2006 World Cup qualification in the European zone with seven goals.

9. On 26 June 2009, Ronaldo signed a contract with Real Madrid and officially joined the club on 1 July 2009.

10. At the age of twenty–two, Ronaldo captained Portugal for the first time.

CRISTIANO RONALDO
MULTIPLE STEP OVERS

The most expensive player in the history of world football set the English Premier League alight with his mind-blowing tricks and technique when he played for Manchester United. Apart from costing the most money, he is one of the most exciting and dynamic players in the world today. This skill is classic Ronaldo and is a trademark move that is synonymous with his name. You need to be going at top speed to pull off this skill.

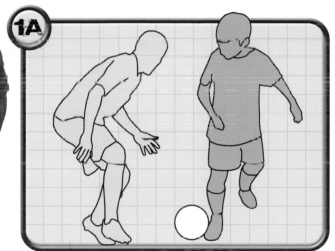

Step 1: As you approach your opponent (1A), pretend to move on your way by flicking your foot over the ball in the direction that you are running (1B), but without actually touching the ball.

Step 2: When your foot goes over the ball, quickly push it in the opposite direction with the inside surface of your foot.

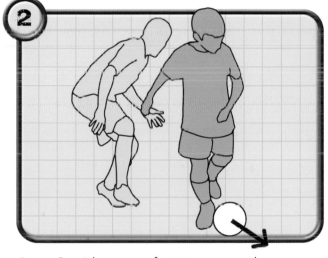

Step 3: Repeat steps one and two until you have wrong-footed your marker.

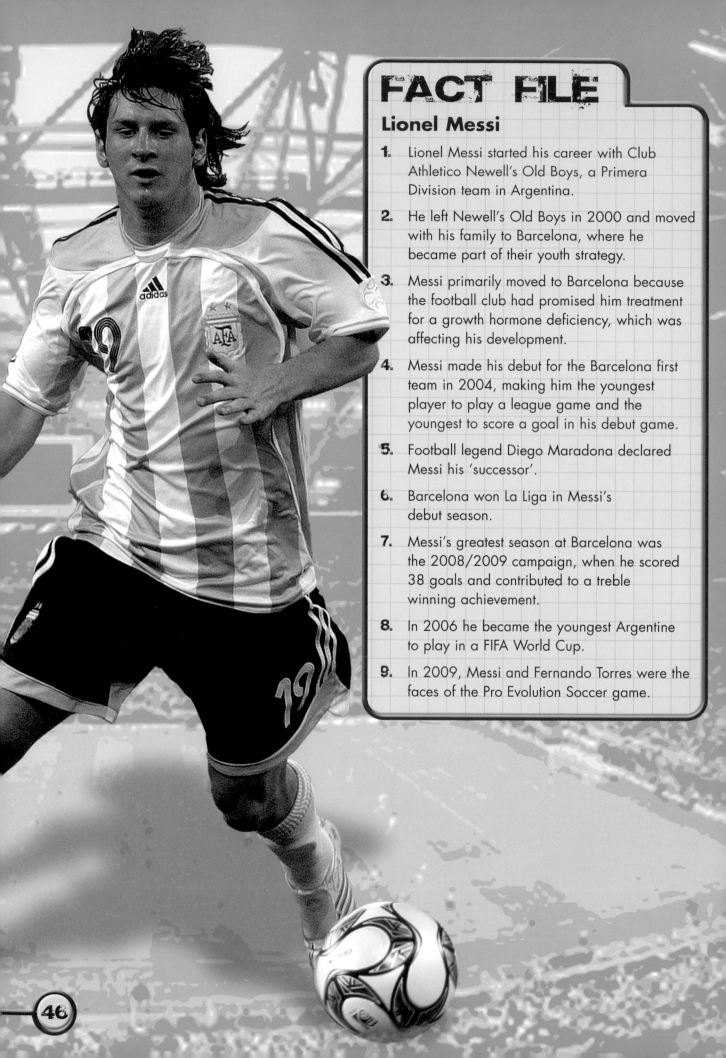

FACT FILE

Lionel Messi

1. Lionel Messi started his career with Club Athletico Newell's Old Boys, a Primera Division team in Argentina.

2. He left Newell's Old Boys in 2000 and moved with his family to Barcelona, where he became part of their youth strategy.

3. Messi primarily moved to Barcelona because the football club had promised him treatment for a growth hormone deficiency, which was affecting his development.

4. Messi made his debut for the Barcelona first team in 2004, making him the youngest player to play a league game and the youngest to score a goal in his debut game.

5. Football legend Diego Maradona declared Messi his 'successor'.

6. Barcelona won La Liga in Messi's debut season.

7. Messi's greatest season at Barcelona was the 2008/2009 campaign, when he scored 38 goals and contributed to a treble winning achievement.

8. In 2006 he became the youngest Argentine to play in a FIFA World Cup.

9. In 2009, Messi and Fernando Torres were the faces of the Pro Evolution Soccer game.

LIONEL MESSI
CROSS DRAG

Lionel Messi's great control and ability to retain possession for vast periods of the game is based on continuous movement of the ball. Just as markers think they can get the ball, Messi has moved it in another direction. The cross-drag is one of the many skills he uses to enrich his vast repertoire.

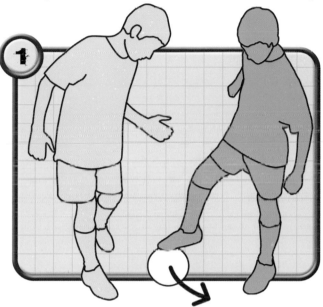

Step 1: As your opponent attempts to make a tackle, drag the ball towards you, using the bottom outside surface of your foot.

Step 2: The drag on the top of the ball will move the ball across your standing leg and away from the path of the interception.

Step 3: As the ball moves beyond your standing leg, you will be able to progress past your opponent.

PRO TIP

As with the ronaldinho skill described earlier in the book on page 35, this move is best executed if you can perform it without looking in the direction that you intend to play the ball. Maintaining eye contact with your opponent will increase your success rate with this move!

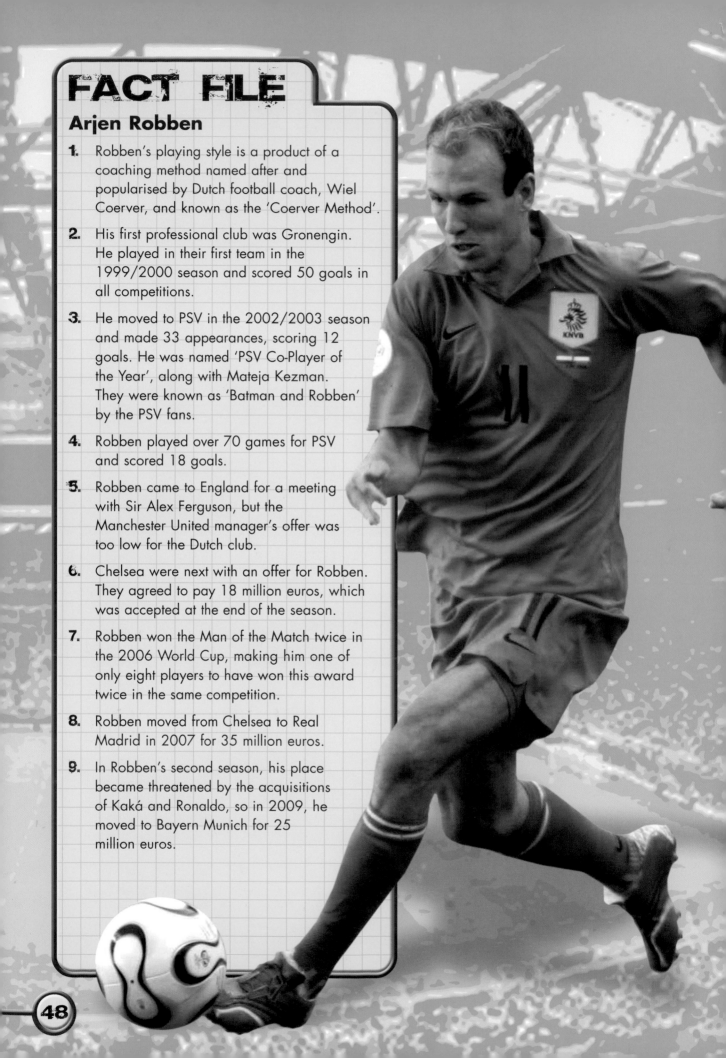

FACT FILE

Arjen Robben

1. Robben's playing style is a product of a coaching method named after and popularised by Dutch football coach, Wiel Coerver, and known as the 'Coerver Method'.

2. His first professional club was Gronengin. He played in their first team in the 1999/2000 season and scored 50 goals in all competitions.

3. He moved to PSV in the 2002/2003 season and made 33 appearances, scoring 12 goals. He was named 'PSV Co-Player of the Year', along with Mateja Kezman. They were known as 'Batman and Robben' by the PSV fans.

4. Robben played over 70 games for PSV and scored 18 goals.

5. Robben came to England for a meeting with Sir Alex Ferguson, but the Manchester United manager's offer was too low for the Dutch club.

6. Chelsea were next with an offer for Robben. They agreed to pay 18 million euros, which was accepted at the end of the season.

7. Robben won the Man of the Match twice in the 2006 World Cup, making him one of only eight players to have won this award twice in the same competition.

8. Robben moved from Chelsea to Real Madrid in 2007 for 35 million euros.

9. In Robben's second season, his place became threatened by the acquisitions of Kaká and Ronaldo, so in 2009, he moved to Bayern Munich for 25 million euros.

ARJEN ROBBEN
CROSS DRAG AND SWIVEL PASS

For a player who mostly occupies wide positions on the pitch, this particular skill is useful when the path forward is blocked by a resolute full back. It enables the advanced wide player to quickly, and with great disguise, pass the ball back to a supporting player in a deeper position.

Step 2: Once the sole of your boot has dragged across the ball and your heel has made contact with the ground, use the outside surface of your foot, combined with a flick from the ankle, to play the ball backwards to a supporting player.

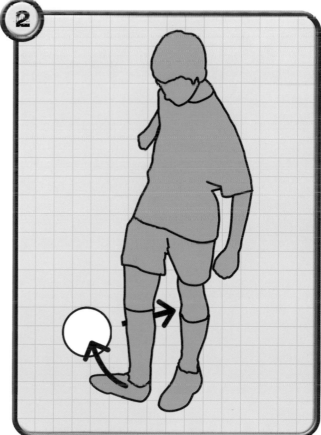

Step 1: Move forward, close to the marking player, and execute the cross-drag skill (see page 47), suggesting that you are going to continue your efforts to get goal side of him.

PRO TIP
The key to this skill is maintaining your cool. Keep eye contact with your opponent as you drag the ball across, and they will be completely surprised by this simple, but effective skill.

FACT FILE

Thierry Henry

1. Henry was born in Les Ulis, Essone, a tough neighbourhood of Paris and played for several amateur sides, before being spotted by AS Monaco in 1990.

2. It took four years for Henry to make his professional debut and another four years before he gained international recognition.

3. Henry is Arsenal's all-time leading scorer with 226 goals in all competitions.

4. He was named PFA Player's Player of the Year twice & the Football Writers' Association Footballer of the Year three times, while playing for Arsenal.

5. He spent two years as club captain at Arsenal.

6. Henry was the top goalscorer for every season that he was a player there.

7. Henry was transferred to Barcelona from Arsenal for a fee of 24 million euros.

8. He is an active campaigner in football's fight against racism.

9. In 2007, he surpassed Michel Platini's record to become France's top goalscorer of all time.

THIERRY HENRY

SCISSORS PASS BEHIND STANDING FOOT

Like all great players, Henry has many skills that he can use to get himself out of a tight situation. This skilful manoeuvre has left many defenders standing, just when they thought they had this dynamic French forward exactly where they wanted him.

Step 1: With the ball still, or nearly still, pretend that you are going to play the ball with your foot that is closest to the bye-line.

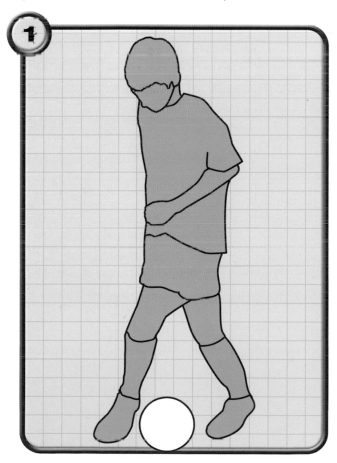

PRO TIP
This skill is best used when the ball is still and a player has very little room to manoeuvre.

Step 2: Instead of playing the ball with your front foot, jump towards the ball, planting your standing foot at least 9 inches in front of the ball. As your standing foot lands, bring your following foot through, contacting the ball with the front of your foot and lifting it in the direction of the goal or a teammate.

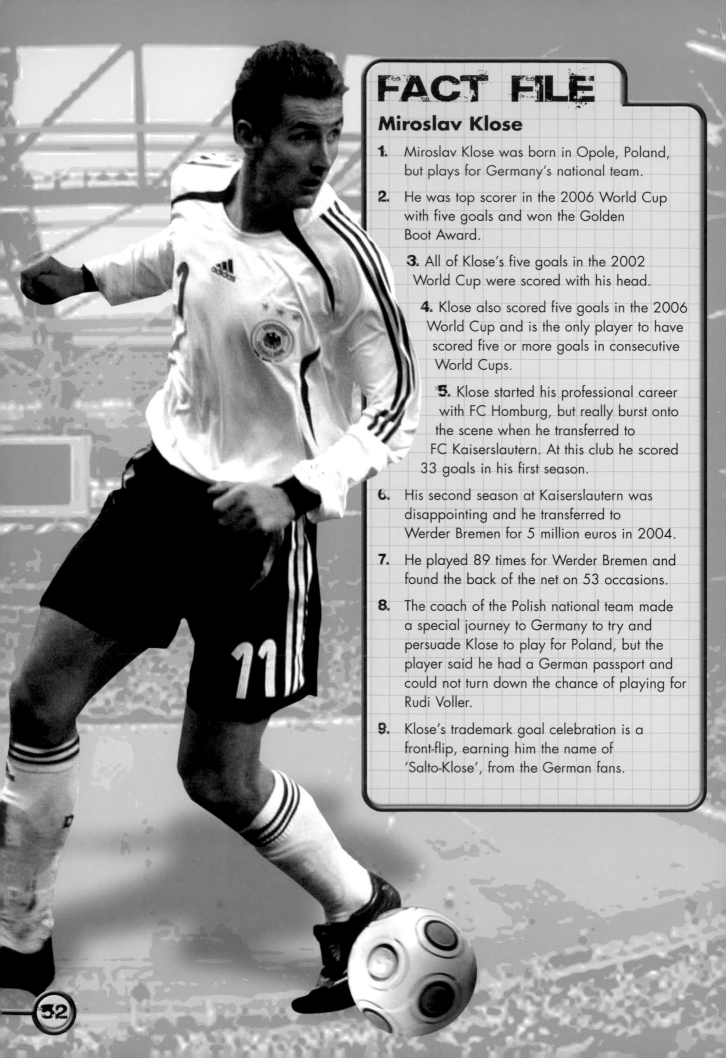

FACT FILE

Miroslav Klose

1. Miroslav Klose was born in Opole, Poland, but plays for Germany's national team.

2. He was top scorer in the 2006 World Cup with five goals and won the Golden Boot Award.

3. All of Klose's five goals in the 2002 World Cup were scored with his head.

4. Klose also scored five goals in the 2006 World Cup and is the only player to have scored five or more goals in consecutive World Cups.

5. Klose started his professional career with FC Homburg, but really burst onto the scene when he transferred to FC Kaiserslautern. At this club he scored 33 goals in his first season.

6. His second season at Kaiserslautern was disappointing and he transferred to Werder Bremen for 5 million euros in 2004.

7. He played 89 times for Werder Bremen and found the back of the net on 53 occasions.

8. The coach of the Polish national team made a special journey to Germany to try and persuade Klose to play for Poland, but the player said he had a German passport and could not turn down the chance of playing for Rudi Voller.

9. Klose's trademark goal celebration is a front-flip, earning him the name of 'Salto-Klose', from the German fans.

MIROSLAV KLOSE

PASS RECEIVED AND SWIVEL RETURN

This great German player is a prolific striker, and it is the art of being able to operate in crowded penalty areas that has helped him to achieve such an enviable goal-scoring record on the world stage.

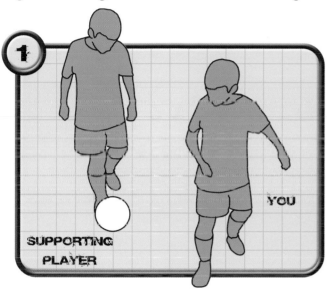

Step 1: You should be running towards the goal without the ball, looking for a pass from a supporting player.

Step 2: As the ball approaches you, allow it to pass between your legs.

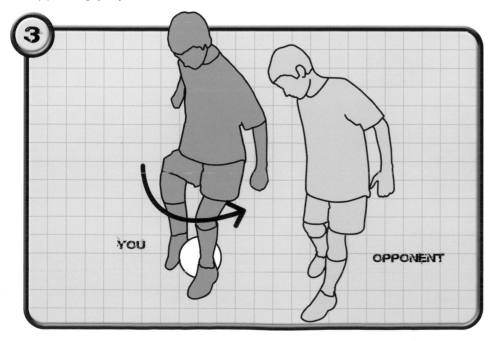

Step 3: At this point, swivel 180 degrees with your dominant foot, taking the ball back inside your standing foot. You are now ready to set off at a different angle from your original run, allowing you to find space and take a shot.

FACT FILE

David Beckham

1. David Beckham was born on 2nd May, 1975 in Leytonstone, London.

2. He is the only English player – and the 21st player, regardless of nationality – to score in three World Cups.

3. Beckham founded the David Beckham Academy in 2005 – a football school in London and Los Angeles. Further Academy sites are planned for the future.

4. He was the first England captain to be sent off and the first England player ever to receive two red cards.

5. Beckham made his first-team debut for Manchester United in 1992, aged seventeen.

6. Beckham was awarded an OBE (Order of the British Empire) for his services to football in June 2003.

7. In 1996, Beckham scored a spectacular goal from the halfway line against Wimbledon. He scored from his own half again in 2008, playing for LA Galaxy.

8. When Beckham signed for Real Madrid, he decided to wear shirt number 23. He said this was due to his admiration of basketball legend Michael Jordon, who wore the number also.

9. Beckham made his first appearance for the England national football team on 1st September, 1996, in a World Cup qualifying match against Moldova.

DAVID BECKHAM
OUTSIDE FOOT FLICK, TURN AND SHOT

This world class player has great technique when it comes to beating markers. This is one of the techniques that he uses to get goalside when under great pressure.

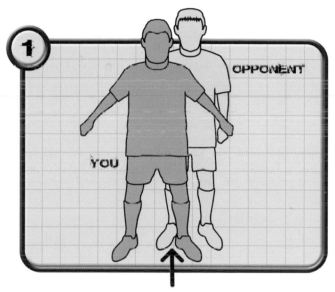

Step 1: Position your body so that you are shielding the approaching ball from your marker.

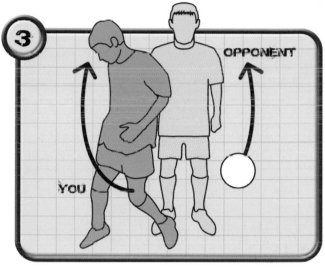

Step 2: As the ball arrives, flick the inside surface of the ball with the outside edge of your boot sending it behind you, and around your marker.

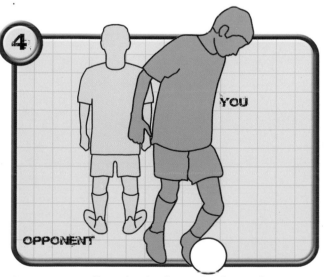

Step 3: Turn and run past your marker on the opposite side that you flicked the ball.

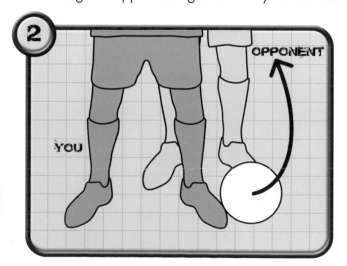

Step 4: Collect the ball, and take a shot on goal in the space that you have created.

FACT FILE

Andréas Iniesta

1. England national player, Wayne Rooney, believes Iniesta is the best midfield player in the world.

2. Iniesta enlisted for the Barcelona Youth School at the age of twelve.

3. He is a utility player, in every sense of the word, and can play in most positions on the pitch. He played as a striker in two Champions League games and found the back of the net twice.

4. Iniesta's first international call to represent Spain was in the 2006 World Cup.

5. He has steered Barcelona to three La Liga Championships since 2004, won the Copa del Rey 2008/2009, the UEFA Champions League 2005/2006 & 2008/2009, and the UEFA Super Cup in 2009.

6. Sir Alex Ferguson once said of Iniesta and his fellow midfielder Xavi: 'I don't think Iniesta and Xavi have ever given the ball away'.

7. In the 2008 European Championships, Iniesta was recorded as having made 254 passes in the tournament with an 89 per cent success rate, so Sir Alex was nearly right.

8. The first goal Iniesta ever scored for Spain was against England, in a friendly, in February 2007.

ANDRÉAS INIESTA
THE SWAY

This neat and tidy midfield general of the Spanish national team has perfected the art of keeping opponents guessing, until the last moment, where he is going to play the ball. This is a great skill for tempting opponents to commit themselves and make foolhardy tackles.

Step 1: The ball has to be on the ground and positioned between your feet.

Step 2: Rock from side to side (2A), accentuating your body movement in the direction you are NOT (2B) going to play the ball.

Step 3: Continue making this movement until one of your feints tempts the opponent to make a challenge, at which point you move off in the opposite direction.

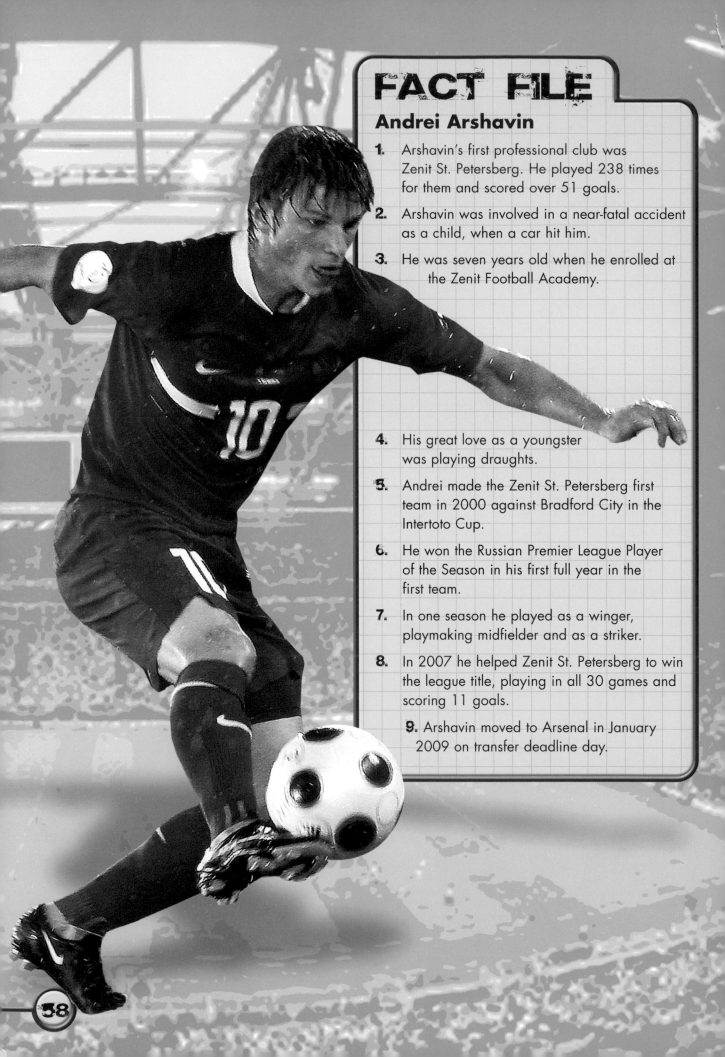

FACT FILE

Andrei Arshavin

1. Arshavin's first professional club was Zenit St. Petersberg. He played 238 times for them and scored over 51 goals.

2. Arshavin was involved in a near-fatal accident as a child, when a car hit him.

3. He was seven years old when he enrolled at the Zenit Football Academy.

4. His great love as a youngster was playing draughts.

5. Andrei made the Zenit St. Petersberg first team in 2000 against Bradford City in the Intertoto Cup.

6. He won the Russian Premier League Player of the Season in his first full year in the first team.

7. In one season he played as a winger, playmaking midfielder and as a striker.

8. In 2007 he helped Zenit St. Petersberg to win the league title, playing in all 30 games and scoring 11 goals.

9. Arshavin moved to Arsenal in January 2009 on transfer deadline day.

ANDREI ARSHAVIN
THE SCREEN TURN DRIBBLE

This fast, powerful forward is renowned for his explosive forays into enemy territory and changing the shape of the game with one masterful move. The 'screen turn dribble' is one such move.

Step 1: Dribble with the ball using the outside surface of your feet. This will generate greater speed, as compared to using the inside surfaces of your feet.

Step 2: When your opponent is matching your pace, any attempt to go past them whilst showing them the ball, is risky.

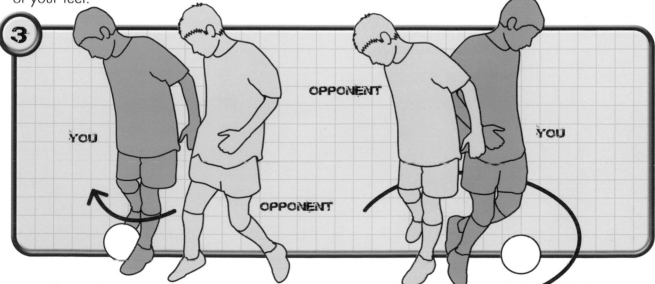

Step 3: At the point where you are rapidly approaching the bye-line move between the ball and your opponent, and turn full circle. Whilst the sight of the ball is blocked, take it behind your opponent with your inside foot surface and continue on your run.

FACT FILE

Patrice Evra

1. Evra was born in Dakar, Senegal, but plays for the French national team.

2. He began his career at the same club as Thierry Henry.

3. Evra was a winger when he played for Paris Saint-Germain and a striker when he played for Nice in Ligue 2.

4. Didier Deschamps, the manager of AS Monaco, at the time, signed Evra from Nice, for an undisclosed fee.

5. Evra signed for Manchester United in January 2006 for a fee of 5.5 million pounds, on a three-year contract.

6. Evra established himself as a first team regular in the 2007/2008 season, making 47 appearances and helping United clinch their second successive Premier League title.

PATRICE EVRA
THE AERIAL DRIBBLE

Evra is famed for his lung-busting forays up the pitch. He is a great juggler of the ball and we are all waiting for the day when one of his charges is executed without the ball touching the ground. This is a very high level skill and even at professional level it is doubtful that many players could beat more than two markers using it.

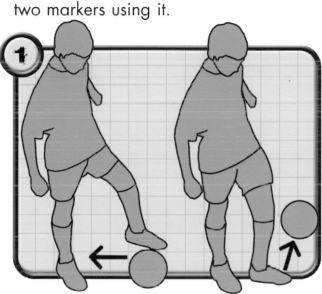

Step 1: Get the ball into the air by pulling the ball back and flicking it into the air.

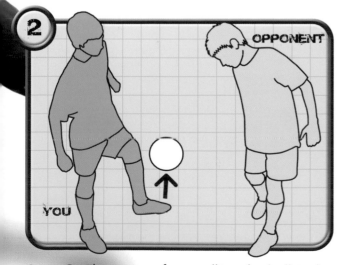

Step 2: The secret of controlling the ball in the air is not to allow it to go too high. Ideally, no more than a foot away from your controlling foot is ideal, until you are near a marker.

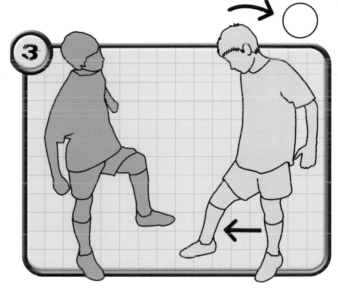

Step 3: Either play the ball over the head of your opponent or to the side, but still in the air.

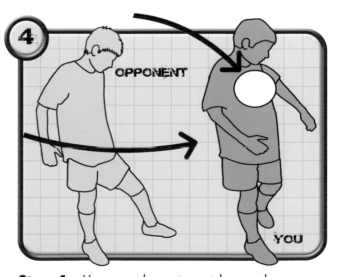

Step 4: You now have to get beyond your opponent and contact the ball while it is still in the air. This is easier said than done!

61

FACT FILE

Nicolas Anelka

1. Nicolas Anelka has played for nine different professional clubs.

2. He only played ten games for his first professional club, PSG, before moving to Arsenal in 1997. He played 65 games for Arsenal and scored 23 goals.

3. He was PFA Young Player of the Year in his second season at Arsenal.

4. Real Madrid signed him for 22.3 million pounds in 1999 – a record fee at that time.

5. He never settled at Real Madrid and was brought back to PSG in a 20 million pound deal.

6. Anelka hankered after Premier League football and his next move was a loan deal with Liverpool. It was a brief association, consisting of 20 games and only four goals.

7. At the start of the 2002/2003 season, Anelka left Liverpool for Manchester City in a 13 million pound deal.

8. After playing for Fenerbahçe in Turkey and then moving back to England to play for Bolton, he finally ended up at Chelsea, in a 15 million pound transfer deal.

9. His transfer value over the years has amounted to 90 million pounds, making him the second most expensive player in the world, second only to Cristiano Ronaldo.

NICOLAS ANELKA

SOLE PULL AND PUSH BEHIND STANDING LEG

Anelka's speed of thought and action makes him one of the most dangerous attackers in the English Premier League and a big favourite with fans.

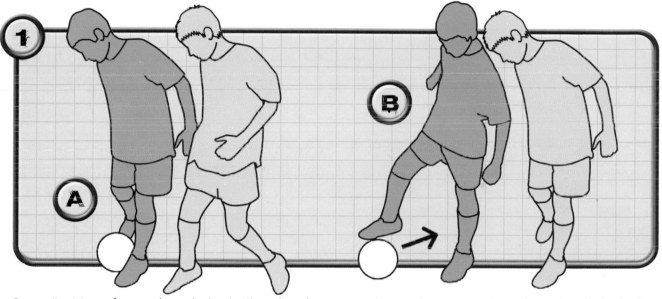

Step 1: Move forwards with the ball under close control (A). Then, stop abruptly and pull the ball back towards you, using the sole of your foot (B).

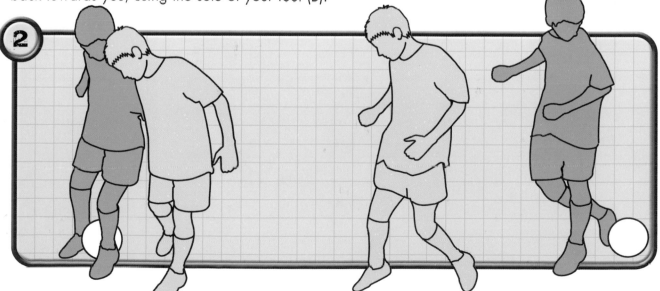

Step 2: In one smooth movement, use the inside surface of your controlling foot to direct the ball behind your standing foot, as a pass or as part of an onward dribble.

CONCLUSION

Don't forget that the skills the world-class players use to stamp their brilliance on the game had to be learnt. Ronaldo didn't just have the innate talent to be able to run with the ball, using step-overs, the first time he ever came into contact with a football. He had to practice and practice until it became something he could instinctively produce. The audacious flicks and back-foot traps, the inside-the-standing-foot passes and the sole of the foot techniques all had to be honed to a level of perfection, which ensured that they could be used in a competitive environment.

Whilst players like Ronaldo, Ronaldinho and Berbatov were practising these skills, they were enjoying themselves. This is the fun side of football; the creative, sunny side of a game that does have its relentless, uncompromising moments. Therefore, it is important that you enjoy practising the skills described in this book, and do not get frustrated if you have difficulty pulling them off.

The satisfaction players and spectators get from that unique moment of skill, which steps outside the workmanlike aspects of the game, is what lifts the spirits of the performer and observer alike. Importantly, we should never forget the greater the influence a player can exert over the ball, the more likely he or she is, to develop into a complete all-round player.

ABOUT THE AUTHOR

Dave Spurdens joined Crystal Palace as a youth player, but after four years with the club was forced to stop playing through injury. He later returned to playing as a semi-professional for a variety of clubs.

Dave is a fully qualified FA Coach and a Physical Education and English teacher.

He has staffed FA coaching courses and was a coach in London schools for twelve years. Dave has also coached in the old Isthmian League.

For many years, he was a freelance football journalist and is the author of many books that have a sporting theme, including Bridgewood High FC, a fictional football trilogy, which was published last year.